This book belongs to:

To Michelle, Paola, Davide and Emily ♥

Author: Serena Lane Ferrari (www.serenalaneferrari.com)
Illustrator: Camilla Frescura (www.behance.net/CamillaFrescura)
Published by Save the Planet Books

First Printing, 2020
ISBN: 979-12-200-6162-9

STINKY SUPER SKUNK

Written by
Serena Lane Ferrari

Illustrated by
Camilla Frescura

Stinky lived in the forest near the great oak tree.
Poor Stinky found it hard to make friends because he often went
–Pffffsss!–
and a stinky poof popped out.

Young Stinky is learning to control his
special stinky skills.
Stinky did stinky poofs when he walked
–Pffffsss!
He did stinky poofs when he ate
–Pffffsss!

When he saw the squirrels playing
acorn-ball, he tried to join in.
But in the middle of the game
-Pffffsss!
A stinky poof popped out.

When Stinky visited Mr and Mrs Mouse
for a cup of tea
-Pffffsss!
A stinky poof popped out.

When Stinky helped Mrs Rabbit walk
her twelve little bunnies to school
–Pffffsss!
A stinky poof popped out.

When Stinky had a bath, stinky
bubbles popped out of the water!
The beavers rushed out the stream.

One day, Mr Owl called a meeting
at the old tree stump.
All the animals from the forest were invited.
All except Stinky.
“The time has come to get rid of that Stinky,”
said Mr Owl.
“He makes everything smell. He has to go.”
The other creatures nodded.

The next day, the hedgehogs
led Stinky out of the woods.
They took him to the prairie
where Stinky would be all alone.
"You can't upset anyone here,"
said the hedgehogs.
"You can do as many stinks as you like!"

Then they left him and went back to the forest.
Poor Stinky curled up and watched the forest.

Mrs Rabbit was struggling with her twelve bunnies, a tear rolled down Stinky's cheek. The squirrels were playing acorn-ball, Stinky sobbed...

Until

-BANG
-BANG
-BANG!

He heard a terrifying blast!

Animals ran riot.
Birds flew wildly in the sky.

The mouse family didn't
know where to hide.
Fox ran for his life.

Wolf protected her pups in a cave.

BANG-BANG-BANG!

“The hunters are here!”
Mrs Rabbit screamed.
“Quick, quick! Hide, hide!”
Mr Owl hooted in reply.

The hunters shot their guns at anything that moved. The whole forest was in a panic. Stinky could hardly believe his eyes and ears.

His friends were in danger.
He had to help them.
And he knew exactly what to do.
Stinky scampered close to the horrible
hunters and hid in a bush.

Then... on your mark... get set...
-PFFFFSSS!
He popped out the biggest, stinkiest stinky poof ever!

PFFFFSSS!
He did it again!
PFFFFSSS, PFFFFSSS, PFFFFSSS!
Stinky kept going, on and on, until
he had no more strength.

A disgusting smell surrounded the hunters!
They couldn't breathe.
They couldn't see.
They coughed, and they choked.

At last, they dropped their guns
and ran out of the forest.
Out of the land.
Far, far away, never to be seen again!

The animals tumbled out of their hiding places.
"You are our hero, Stinky!" they shouted.
They cuddled him and they hugged him.

“We’re so sorry for how we treated you,” they said. “Please, please come back. You’ve saved us all. You’re a super skunk!” The animals threw a welcome-home party for Stinky that went on all night long.

Stinky has learnt that being unique has its advantages

STINKY SUPER SKUNK

Coloring pages

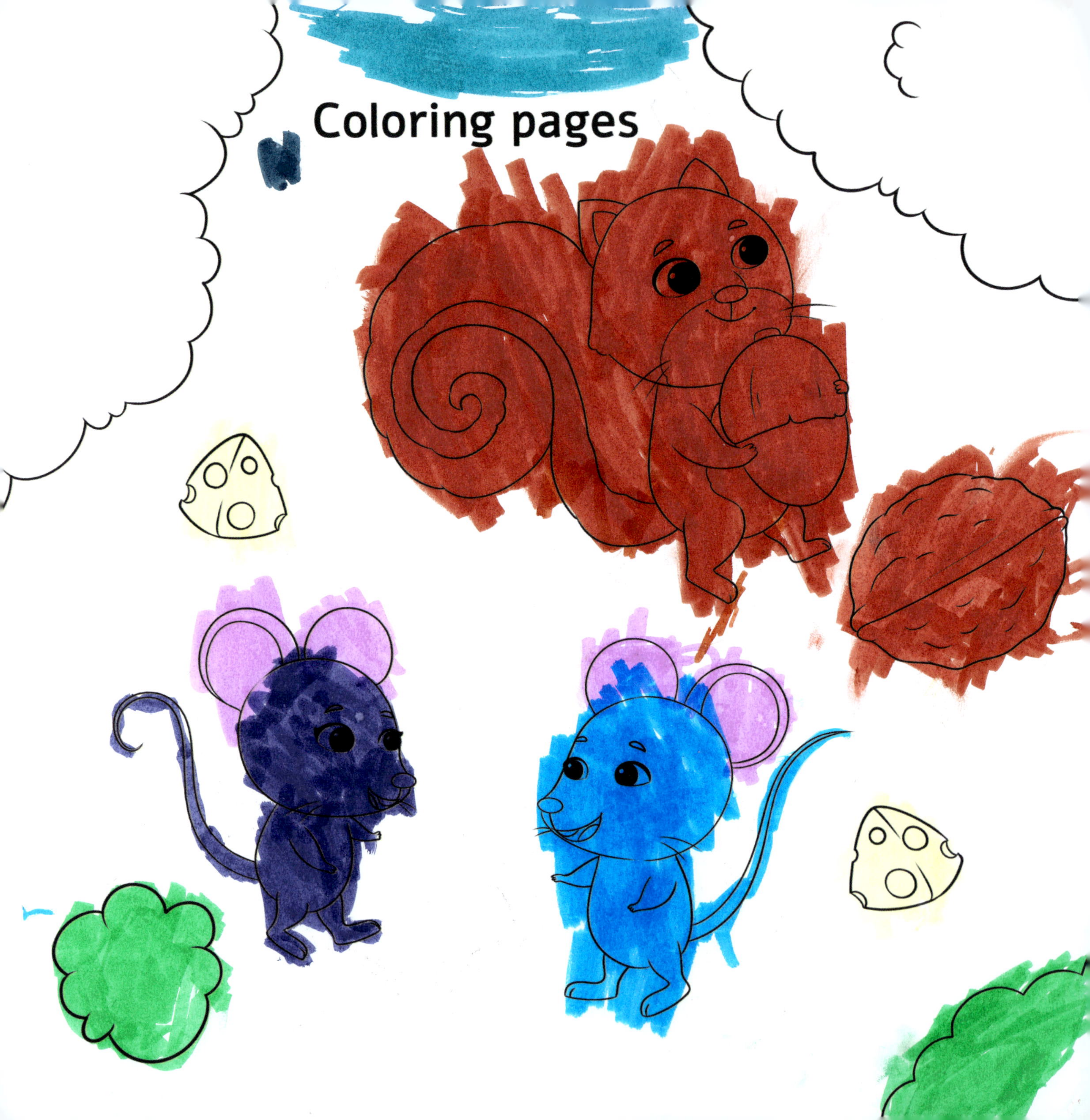

STINKY
SUPER
SKUNK

We proudly support

treedom®

let's green the planet

Reforestation is the most
effective method to fight climate change

Serena Lane Ferrari   Camilla Frescura

You buy books, we plant trees.

From the Author

I write books for young children that have the **future of our planet** at their heart. I passionately believe that children are our last chance to improve our ecosystems, find solutions to major climate problems, and save the planet.

I also believe in the importance of **reading to children** from an early age, and hope that my books engage children (and parents!) and inspire them to believe in a better future.

I love hearing from readers, and welcome you to **interact with me** on facebook (www.facebook.com/SerenaLaneFerrari) or to **contact me** at serenalaneferrari@gmail.com

Would you mind taking a few seconds to leave a review of my book? It's important because **your opinion** helps people make better decisions.

Thank you!

Serena Lane Ferrari

Sneak Peek

Did You Steal my MILK?

A Journey into Plant Based Dairy Alternatives

Who has stolen the milk? Unicorns?

Dragons wearing uniforms? The bat dangling from a hat?

The green bug playing with a slug?

Emma asks the whole farm about her missing breakfast drink, and learns that the true culprit might be herself.

Jingo in the Jungle

Saving the Jewels of the Earth

JINGO the orangutan loves his beautiful jungle habitat — but when bulldozers arrive, can he and his animal friends band together to save their home?

Venture deep into the rainforest with this vividly illustrated picture book!

Parents will enjoy an engaging story that speaks directly to kids showing what **deforestation** can do on animals and wildlife habitats.

Children will love reading about Jingo and his brave friends!

Jingo in the Jungle is based on the true story of an orangutan - in Indonesia - defending its home and habitat from being destroyed by a bulldozer.

The Hidden Spaceship

A Journey into Environmental Awareness

When Amelia and Noah stumble across a spaceship, an out-of-this-world adventure begins. The friends have a very special mission - **to help save the Earth's ecosystem**. They must go on a daunting journey on another planet, find a treasure chest, and complete their quest. What secret does the treasure chest hold?

Saving Tally

An Adventure into the Great Pacific Plastic Patch

Tally is a curious little turtle with a talent for getting into trouble.

Her best friend Ara is a wise and strong lobster.

The most dangerous part of the ocean is about to shock Tally and Ara and make them realise that their underwater world isn't always charming. Will they be able to escape the danger?

An engaging book that addresses the issue of **plastic pollution** and how it impacts our oceans and sea life.

Printed in Great Britain
by Amazon

46432105R00024